THE INDUSTRIALISTS' AID TO
FOREIGN EXPANSION AND DEVELOPMENT

THE INDUSTRIALISTS

FOREIGN EXPANSION

A technical guidebook by

AMBROSE J. HARTNETT

ID TO

ND DEVELOPMENT

Foreword

This work is directed to and intended for the industrial appetite of the domestic entity, corporate or individual, which is stomached and sufficiently intrepid to advance its industrial activities and efforts into the foreign field.

Intelligent and well-guided expansion in the newly opened, and even the oldly existing, areas of foreign operation can, and very well may, realize even greater and more permanent financial rewards and protected profits than could be anticipated in many cases from home operations.

The author does not presume his reader necessarily to be an amateur in the field; rather does he trust that his own experiences as international banker, private consultant, and personal investor, will to some extent contribute in a seasoned way—let us say, add flavor—to the perhaps even vaster and more learned experience of those—corporate or individual—who may have traveled the trail of foreign industrial development farther than has he.

To the uninitiated, we bid "welcome," and hope that for them this work will have definitive value.

Ambrose J. Hartnett
527 Lexington Avenue
New York 17, N. Y.
U. S. A.
December 22, 1963

Contents

THE INDUSTRIALISTS' AID TO
FOREIGN EXPANSION AND DEVELOPMENT

1 Introduction

In this modern day arena of international pugilistics, political propaganda, and illogical economic reprisals, the industrialist is thoroughly dismayed, conceivably well confused, and irrevocably stagnated in his corporate thoughts, words, and deeds.

His home market is saturated with competition, often destroyed by shrewdly copied import varieties, and inundated by backwashes of overdevelopment and underconsumption. Supply and Demand, once touted as economic law, are no longer a balance but an unpredictable metronome swinging to the wild staccata of advertising, public relations, and so called visual media.

Synthesism has replaced realism.

Sweat, brains, and patience are no longer the ingredients of successful achievement. Opportunism, expediency and flash profit are the substitutes.

Many good names, many fine old names, corporately speaking, remain. But how many, appallingly how very many have disappeared, not too few victimized by new disciples of finance and industry, destroyed by insatiable and devouring lusts for rainbow profits, individual prestige, and personal power through simulated corporate strength.

Thoroughly refreshing is the wholesome departure from all this, total or partial, with the advent into virgin territories awaiting industrial development with sound promise of fruitful return.

Leave your competition behind—far behind, even forgotten—eliminate the devastation of confiscatory taxation, thrill to the accomplishment of corporate or personal creative ability, grow your corporate melons where only you may slice them and no others may plunder, select your labor without restraint or constraint, serve a public which serves you, operate without harassment of regulation and control, and reap during the day without the need of tranquilizer at night.

Utopia? Realistically, yes, and it may be possessed by intelligent, planned, well-guided, decisive expansion into the *selective* foreign industrial field.

Admittedly, Utopias can and have become Nemeses, Jekylls darken into Hydes, meat today may be poison tomorrow.

It is for this reason we employ the qualification "*selective*" in relation to "foreign industrial field." The Nemeses, Hydes, and poisons need not have existed, in the main, had selective action been exercised in the first place and maintained, in the second, with wisdom, prudence, and unhesitant courage.

2 The Country

The country selected for your expansion and development program should be *politically*, *socially* and *economically* eligible. It must be acceptable not only to you, individually or corporately, but you must equally be acceptable to it. It need not necessarily be persona-grata to your own country of basic operation, although this could help, no doubt.

POLITICALLY

The country must be susceptible to—if not currently capable of—rule by the people. This, in the author's opinion and experience, is the criterion. Democracies, Dictatorships, Republics—all are styles without fixed meaning or permanent significance in the fast tempo of contemporary politics and, if applied today to a designated country, may incorrectly be so applied tomorrow. Paradoxically and frequently, yesterday's Democracy is today's Military Junta, tomorrow's Dictatorship, and next week's Republic. It is the political comedy—tragedy, perhaps—of this our century of proclaimed "Advanced Civilization."

The fact remains, however, that while forms of government may be transient, the country itself survives and its people remain. The trick is to select the country where you will not be unreasonably

5

vulnerable to political change and where you may ride the troughs as well as the crests. This is quite possible and, with patience, most rewarding.

The author has very definitely experienced superior results in countries of national dictatorship. The reasons for this are unmistakable.

The dictator inevitably is a forceful man, but a man of internal fears. He may be motivated by pure love of country or he, perhaps, may have a thirst for personal power, with attendant vices of corruption and aggrandizement. No matter the forces that propel him, he is or soon becomes emotionally unstable, privately at first, publicly at times. He, if a military man, discovers his inadequacy in economics, finance, administration; if nonmilitary, he will be political species and no less vulnerable in the same areas. Neither military nor political will survive without quickly and surely consolidating his position. This requires doing, in addition to promising, more for his people than his predecessor if he is to remain in business. Otherwise, he goes too!

For this understandable reason, the dictator welcomes external influences which will shore up his national economy, happy the people through employment, contribute to public welfare, and economically medicate the country for strength, peace, and survival. If he accomplishes this, public response is one of loud-throated approbation and many "vivas." The dictator lives for another day and very possibly, in the maturity of his rule might even become a beloved president. This seems to be the general plan, but the important factor is that, whether or not the plan works, it does open the door to outside industry and provide remarkably robust opportunity for expansion and development. In this atmosphere one can expect, and usually receive, speedy negotiation of industrial enterprise, generous concessions, and exhilarating absence of bureaucratic, redundant, red-taped mishmash.

Many readers will recoil, at this point, in strong objection, recalling the long, lingering, and painfully wearing and wearying memory of Cuba. The answer to the objection is more simple than the cure of the ill: the seed that spawned Castro Cuba was, *and is,* more virulent than the Communistic strength that nourished and still maintains it. *Selectivity* may have been applied but it very definitely was not maintained. This is not opinion; it is history. Many industries lost millions of investment dollars in Cuba; far more industrialists recouped their investments and made millions in profits. The losers may have been, the winners remained—selective.

As for self-styled Democracies, Republics, et al.—be selective, as you would in a Dictatorship. Select with an eye to susceptibility to rule by the people.

SOCIALLY

It is stock-in-trade to emphasize that the richest field for industrial development and expansion exists in the underdeveloped, or to be exacting—underprivileged, countries of the world. There you will discover the mass illiterates, the at times staggering primitive conditions, even the dangers of barbaric practice. But, this can be the Utopia—if you are selective. For here you will find vast natural resources inviting industry, surplus labor markets, fantastically untapped consumer demand, genuinely cooperative and honestly sincere government officials.

Illiteracy does not imply mental vacuum. By and far, the illiterates are fundamentally and basically intelligent. They make willing workers, are honest as a group, sober and reliable. Extend them the opportunity to learn, accord them the decencies of humane treatment, and how greatly enriched will be your experience in employee relations. Give them the "privilege" and they will spontaneously shoulder the responsibility, and this will pass from father to son.

Primitive conditions are your challenge to accept, and you must tolerate them only insofar as you are unwilling to correct them, at least in the area of your operation. You are primitive, not the natives, if you cannot bring with you a reasonably simple but effective plan for immediate improvement of local conditions in the matter of sanitation, housing, pest control, and water supply. If you are unwilling or unable to do this, keep out!

In the long run and the short one too, natives are less barbaric than their foreign brothers. Human emotions run deeper beneath their impassive countenances, their suspicions are natural and well founded, their ritual practices long established. Education, in time, will eradicate undesirable traits and beliefs, but care must be exercised that they are not replaced by far more undesirable characteristics of contemporary "civilization."

ECONOMICALLY

Natural resources of land, raw materials supply, fuel, etc., are essential. So, too, is local labor, unskilled substantially, but at commensurate pay levels.

All raw materials need not be found locally, but the substantial and basic ones should, and will, if again you are selective. Imported materials and supplies, to be acceptable, must be readily available and at economically permissible prices.

Labor, in an underprivileged country, is in astonishing surplus supply, cheap rate, and nonunionized, of course. Unskilled labor will flock to your camp by droves, some skilled will be located in nearby community centers. Much unskilled can be effectively trained to semiskilled and even skilled by your imported technicians. Tried and tested, you will undergo considerably less difficulty and trouble here than you did back home. And you will receive vastly more in return.

Consumer demand must be related to population, growth, education, and improvement of living standards. Most selective countries in the underprivileged class will qualify in this respect.

You would be foresighted, it might be injected here, to select

8

your industrial site adjacent to a port facility. Cheaper production costs could readily introduce your product into a lucrative export market, as well.

In all your procedures of negotiation, surveys, studies, and the like, it undoubtedly will surprise you pleasantly to receive considerable cooperation, attention, and action from the officials of government who have been delegated to your assistance. This is the normal and good disposition of these people and they usually ask only *your* success in return. On the other hand, if, as a foreigner accustomed to reading perennial political scandals in your favorite home press, you assume the patronizing role of tycoon in this the foreign land, your patronage will be well exacted—and you asked for it.

The author has negotiated with several of the firmest dictators of this century, has repeatedly been assisted and "protected" by national secret police, been accompanied and completely successfully served by high-ranking cabinet ministers, has procured valid concessions of very substantial value—and has neither paid nor been solicited tribute. Mutual respect and commonly shared motives for human improvement are the secret, if such it may be classified.

3   The Project

If already in domestic industry, your venture into the foreign field
will be an expansion into the foreign market with on-spot production facilities, development of a new product not only for the
market abroad but export home as well, or diversification to entirely
new industry.

The investor—new corporate or individual—not in active business, as yet, will be guided by the very same rules as the veteran
home industrial, except that it or he will exercise greater caution in
selection of desirable project so as not to crawl where others may
run.

An excellent project guide for the existing corporation is its
export market. If this market has been, is, or could be lucrative, by
all means seek out the foremost foreign consumer country—active
or potential—and expand your manufacturing facilities to that re-
gion. With on-spot production and distribution, you will firmly
secure that market, manufacture at cheaper cost, obtain higher
profits, and protect your trade position on long term basis through
prohibitive import tariffs.

A second method, applicable to production diversification, is the
study of long range industrialization programs planned by most of
the new nations, and new developments envisaged by many of the
older countries as well.

Industrial planning, with offers to outside capital of participation in or actual ownership of attractive projects, is widespread among the underdeveloped and lesser developed nations of today's "modern" world. Safely can it be said, few home industries—great or small—will find other than munificent opportunity in actively identifying themselves with this planning—but, selectively, always remember.

You will find really sound national areas—far from your basic domestic operations—with untold manufacturing and marketing potential. The consumer demand will range from sugar to toothpaste, shoes to beer, steel to frozen foods—you name it, it *is* there.

In plotting your project, shrewd consideration will be given to utilization of material from production waste for by-products manufacture. This particularly applies to industries using agricultural raw materials in manufacturing processes. Scientific research and classic accomplishment have physically demonstrated practical values in this area and actual utilizations could create, in some cases, substantially greater profits than those being realized from prime production.

Presuming that you have elected your project and selected your new country of industrial operations, a visit to its territory is now indicated. This trip, unorthodox as it may seem, will best be conducted as a tourist. In this manner you may determine the general condition of the country, associate more freely with the people, travel internally and extensively without formal notice, and quite freely flex your industrial muscles without commitment of exercise. Additionally, you will learn more of political background, personalities, trend of public thought and future action, fears, hopes, and plans of the government and of the populace—all without being suspect. Previous concepts will possibly be amended, modified, or even altogether changed. You might alter your industrial plans radically and to your own greater advantage. This modus operandi —the tourist role—besides being more informative and productive of basic results, will be considerably less expensive than had it been conducted as corporation executive or private investor.

Once this first tour is completed, with copious notes and impressions gained, serious discussions back home are merited with the combined forces you must muster for success of your project. This, of course, presumes positive evaluation.

Preliminary conferences with your Financial Consultant and Consultant Engineers are required. Sufficient financial support, on qualified basis, must be assured now although later secured through the formidable intermediary of the Feasibility Report.

If positive evaluation of project holds, next on the agenda is a return to your foreign base, but this time in company with your Financial Consultant and a small but choice group culled from your Consultant Engineers. With prior recognition and approval of the National Government and its local authorities, conduct the first operation required to establish the feasibility of your project—its economics.

The economics will be evaluated in seven steps:

1. Descriptive
2. Raw Material Supply
3. Labor
4. Preliminary Estimates of Production Costs
5. Evaluation of Market
6. Transportation
7. Taxes

1 DESCRIPTIVE

This will include the location of the country; its political, social, and economic backgrounds and trends; general relationships with border countries; potential for improvement; capability of and susceptibility to rule by the people.

Into this pattern integrate your project, its need and value to the national economy, the manner in which it will function, what it will accomplish.

Bold language should be used in the survey report but not abused to the extent that artistry replaces realism.

2 RAW MATERIAL SUPPLY

Basic raw materials should be of native origin if the project is to be attractive and have financability.

If imports will be required, be assured of their availability at plant delivered costs which will be economically acceptable.

3 LABOR

Native labor will be predominantly unskilled but it should be responsive to proper training, education, and supervision.

It should be, as you know, honest, sober, and reliable.

Pay rates should be commensurate with local conditions and geared to living standards and wage scales observed nationally.

Skilled labor, to some degree, will be found in larger communities and can be supplemented by your own imported technicians.

It is always surprising to discover unusually clever technicians locally available, natives who are superior in many respects to their foreign counterparts. They are intimately better acquainted with peculiarities of terrain, soil, rainfall, erosion processes, water levels, and labor than could be the recently arrived expert.

This is particularly true of native civil engineers and agronomists. You would be well advised to look them up and include them sooner than later on your staff.

4 PRELIMINARY ESTIMATES OF PRODUCTION COSTS

You cannot reasonably be expected, on this trip, to calculate complete and accurate sets of production costs. However, you now should have sufficient opportunity and data which will deliver estimates of costs, supporting the value of your project and providing a rough projection of the financial returns it should realize.

Raw material and labor costs are available; you have a good estimate of your *maximum* capital outlay for plant and facilities. Interest expense and loan amortization charges can be determined; insurance, depreciation, and maintenance charges are no problem.

Based on import values of your finished product and local sales prices, it should not be at all impossible to calculate a reputable sales and income return to shield your total cost of production estimates and gauge their accuracy with proper reserve.

5 EVALUATION OF MARKET

Work from available official import data and, with knowledge of your preliminary production costs, project increased consumer demand based on lower priced product. Further project this estimate for population, education, growth, and increased living standard factors, and, perhaps, export appeal to immediately neighboring countries if so indicated.

Determine quotas, if applicable, and assure your equitable participation in same.

Investigate national purchase and distribution possibilities and Government guarantees of minimum market, annual sale, and escalated price features.

6 TRANSPORTATION

Survey the existing road system and estimate cost per mile transportation of your product to central distribution points and end markets. If cost is excessive, relocate your manufacturing site to where this cost will be cheaper. If you cannot do this and your project is of urgent and substantial value to the National economy, negotiations will be in order for government solution through subsidy or road building grant.

In calculating transportation out, do not overlook haulage in —original plant machinery and equipment, supplies and material, basic and continuing later into operation, as well as replacement parts.

7 TAXES

You have endured confiscation of income back home and you have not traveled afield to suffer this evil further.

You are investing capital, expending monies, assuming substantial debt, sweating hot pore salt, and accepting mental burdens and moral responsibilities to bring this bountiful project to an underprivileged country.

It is not more than reasonable to expect that the beneficiary country will grant you the grand incentive of complete tax exemption for a generous period of time. If this is not so, you must be given substantial exoneration or else receive government guaranteed tax recovery at the retail end. This type of recovery is somewhat awkward, prone to abuse, and is nothing less than a cover for actual exemption.

Taxes, known or unknown, will impair financability and simply and specifically cannot be tolerated until such time as the project has paid out two hundred percent of its capital cost.

Be adamant in your demands in this respect.

4 The Concession

The Author, because of broad experience in the foreign field, firmly refuses to negotiate financings or recognize the intrinsic value of any foreign project that is not fully, completely, and long term supported and protected by a legally constituted, valid, and properly issued concession executed by the National Government of the Country wherein the project is to be located. Selectivity—remember it?—in this respect, cannot be misguided, cajoled into less, or be promised more.

Without a solidly good national concession, no matter how big or small you or your corporation may be, you have exactly nothing, sooner or later. And, when the author speaks of Concession, Constitutional Concession and *not* Presidential Decree is explicitly intended.

On your economic survey tour, you should have drafted a general outline of the concession required, and to this made additions as you progressed in your study, observed along the line of work, and conversationally absorbed from natives and such other sources of information as may have favored you.

It is now appropriate to concretely consider just what attributes your concession should contain and possess to more than adequately satisfy the physical and fiscal requirements of the project, attract financing, and protect market, earnings, and capital investment.

The ingredients of the good Concession are herewith presented. They are fact and, in fact, result from various negotiations of the author with certain foreign governments, the examples submitted being actual articles, as translated from foreign tongues to the English.

CLAUSES

ART. 1. The National Government recognizes, approves and otherwise endorses the admittance of the project into the general classification of industry it shall enjoy.

example

The investment proposal of John Doe to engineer, construct, own, and operate one or more plants for the manufacturing of —— product, in conformity with the provisions set forth in this concession, is hereby accepted by the National Government.

ART. 2. The project is specifically identified, with rights.

example

The investor, John Doe, will have the right to engineer, construct, own, and operate one or more complete plants for the manufacturing of — product, with total annual production of, but not limited to, — units; to own, exploit, and administrate — hectares of land required by the plant or plants mentioned; to own, operate, and administrate all the installations required for the efficient and economical operation of the plant or plants, cultivation and supply of raw materials (specify), storage of raw, in process, and finished materials and products, by-products, and the sale and distribution of same; to exercise full autonomy in the selection and contracting of all engineers, mechanics, laborers, contractors, and suppliers in the

18

protection, engineering, construction, and operation of all works included in the subject of this concession.

ART. 3. Government conveys guarantee relative to real property.

example

The Government recognizes and guarantees in favor of John Doe the right of owning the extension of —— hectares of land suitable for the construction and operation of one or more —— plants with a total annual capacity of, but not limited to, —— units. The extension granted of —— hectares may be acquired from the domain of the State or from private owners, may be comprised in a sole unit that would include the above mentioned extension, or in different lots sufficient to attain the extension authorized in the present concession. In case of lands, required by John Doe, which belong to the domain of the State, their concession will be granted in conformity with the laws concerned. In the case of the lands required belonging to particular and private owners, their acquisition will be regulated by the free agreement of the parties concerned; should John Doe be not able to negotiate direct agreement with the respective owners, at the request of John Doe, the Government will dictate measures for exappropriation, declaring for its case, in the present concession, the public necessity and use for the works that John Doe will realize under the terms of the concession, John Doe paying the correspondent indemnization by law, during which process the Government will adopt the legal measures conducting to avoid that the engineering and construction of the works, including exploitation of the lands, be hindered or suspended.

ART. 4. Selection of lands procedure is defined.

example

The survey for availability of lands exclusively acceptable to John Doe, for the purposes specified in this concession, will be conducted jointly by the Government and John Doe, and for this purpose the Government will appoint, without cost or other charge to John Doe, the necessary technical personnel who may presently be in the employ of the Government and whose services may freely be requisitioned by John Doe. Further, the Government shall freely, and without charge or other obligation, make available to John Doe all the information and studies which it may possess and which may be of value in the conduct of the works encompassed by this concession.

ART. 5. Freedom in Technical Direction.

example

The investor shall enjoy complete autonomy in the technical direction of his works and in everything related to the agricultural, industrial, and commercial aspects of the exploitation, with entire freedom to contract and reduce personnel.

ART. 6. *Tax and Duty Exemptions.*

This is possibly the greatest and most valuable single element in your concession, and upon it will hang in the balance not only the financability of your project but also, once financed and completed, its economic survival.

example

While this concession is in force, the Government grants to the investor the following exemptions and franchises:

a) Complete and full liberation from any and all taxes, duties, levies, or charges (including consular), presently existing or to be created in the future, on all importations of machinery, equipment, implements, supplies and sundries to be utilized in the engineering, construction, and *operation* of the project works, and its complete facilities, which are subject of this concession.

b) Complete and total exemption from any and all income and other taxes, imports, duties, tariffs, whatever their class and nomination may be, presently existing or to be created in the future, national, departmental, and municipal, is granted to the investor, individual and corporate, to all his officers, employees, and technicians, of whatever national origin, for the entire period of this concession.

This total and complete exemption applies likewise, in equal force, to all dividends or distributions of monies or values to be declared or made by the investor, corporate or individual; to capital repatriations, payments of loans and interests thereon, purchases and sales of stock in the enterprise, patents, rights, and income of any and all nature.

Likewise, this exemption applies fully and completely to any and all taxes, levies, imports, tariffs, fees, other charges and the like, of whatsoever nature and nomination, existing or to be created in the future, on real estate: purchased, owned, leased, sold or transferred; equipment, machinery, chattels, transfers of stock, personal properties, values, and possessions, without restriction and whether herein specified or not.

ART. 7.   Repatriation of Capital and Earnings.

example

While this concession is in force, the Government firmly and completely guarantees to the investor prompt repatriation of total capital investment, together with all earnings, both as realized, dividends, loan payments and amortizations, loan interest, salaries, monied benefits, proceeds from sales of scrap and obsolete machinery and equipment, profits, and the like, whether herein specified or not, and ready and free convertibility of national currency to U.S.A. dollars.

ART. 8.   Guarantee of Minimum Market (if applicable).

example

The Government guarantees that the sale price (f.o.b. factory) in the internal market, up to (specify) units in annual production, in no case whatsoever shall be less than the manufacturer's costs: production, administration, and general, including loan amortizations and interest expenses, sinking fund reserve requirements, and depreciation, to the total of which shall be added a percentage of profit for the enterprise of not less than (specify) percent; and the Government does likewise hereby guarantee to the investor the sale of (specify) units annually in the internal market.

ART. 9.   Protected Market.

example

The Government, with the object of protecting (specify) industry, subject of this concession, will adopt the necessary measures to suspend the addition of competitive industry in the country for the entire period of this concession, insofar as the country's internal market is satisfied by the production of the investor, and the Government will furthermore suspend all importations of competitive products for the same duration of time insofar as the investor's supply is adequate and sufficient.

ART. 10.   Social Responsibility.

example

The investor will comply with the obligations and duties to his employees and workers which are dictated by the tenets of good society, will stimulate their standards of living by media of education, medical attention and care through his proper facilities, and technical training and instruction for workers selected by him as qualified.

22

ART. 11.   Transfer of Concession.

example

The investor, with previous notice to the Government, shall have the right to transfer, at any time, totally or partially, the concession itself and the rights and duties emanating from it, to one or more juridical persons, with the purpose that this or these will execute the concession and, in this case, they will assume all the rights and obligations of the concession without exception or limitation.

ART. 12.   Political Risk Guarantees.

example

It is expressly covenanted that the Government will cooperate with the investor in all proceedings aiming to obtain policies of guarantee, institutional or from his own Government, insuring his investment against risks from war and exappropriation, and for currency convertibility. The Government will furthermore promptly grant the approvals which may be necessary for the obtaining and possession of such guarantees and policies by the investor.

ART. 13.   Force Majeure.

example

The duration period of this concession will be automatically extended due to the occasion of any fortuitous events, happenings, or incidents which may in any way, manner, or form, delay, harm, or otherwise impair the engineering, construction, ownership, or operation of the project which is the subject of this concession, including land selection and any and all such facilities as may be necessary to the project, without limitation and whether herein specified or not.

In event of such occasion, the investor shall promptly notify the Government of such delays, impairments, or hurts, in writing, and a record will be subscribed of same and extension made to the duration period of this concession.

ART. 14.   Utilization of Public and Private Highways, etc.

example

During the term of this concession the investor is fully and lawfully authorized to operate all forms of transportation required by his project and may freely, without cost to himself, utilize all highways, roads, bridges, viaducts, tunnels, ingresses, egresses, and the like, whether public or privately owned, without limitation or restriction, and in pursuit of the works which are subject of this concession.

The investor may also own and operate, without limitation or restriction, aircraft, telephone and radio services, boats and other craft of water navigation, enjoying free transit over all rivers, lakes, streams, internal waterways, and coastal seas.

ART. 15.   Plant Security.

example

The investor reserves to himself the right to control the entrance of persons to his camps and industrial works and zone except in the case of express authorization of competent authority.

ART. 16.   Subsidiary Industries.

example

The investor may develop subsidiary industries for utilization of by-products from manufacturing processes of the project which is subject of this concession and such subsidiary industries will be included within the full and complete encompassment of this concession, enjoying all the rights of same and undertaking the same obligations.

ART. 17.   Term of Concession.

example

The term of this concession shall be for an uninterrupted duration of twenty-five years, in addition to the period of time required for land selection and plant engineering, construction, and start-up operations, which term may be extended for a second twenty-five years upon the option of the investor.

The foregoing features, as illustrated by actual examples, do not constitute the entirety of a solidly good concession but provide the reader with a balanced framework within which he may construct the requirements peculiar to his own specific project.

The author has developed these features, which are flexible, and adapted them with ease to his negotiations with foreign nations— with considerable success.

Various essential additions, conforming to the nature of your project and its style of operation, should be introduced and relentlessly retained over any and all objections which might be entertained by the National Government.

5 Negotiation of the Concession

Negotiation of the concession is a delicate maneuver, requiring the utmost in diplomacy with firmness; harshness and gentility; conviction not persuasion; and maximum application of basic human psychology. It is distinctly for the expert, not the amateur.

There are many approaches to this negotiation but the author, after years of seasoned and fruitful experience, has found only one that, for him, can securely be identified as effective. Therefore, this system is advanced and recommended. Simply stated, it is this: "Start at the top, then work up."

To turn the clock back for a space: on your first trip to project country as "tourist," maintain your decorum in character and avoid officials of government, the petty as well as the formidable, back in your own country from the start, and now in this new industrial world of yours. Obtain periodicals and maps, read brochures about the land and its people, question the citizenry on arrival, during your internal travel. Solicit information commercially where you may without suspicion of interest; make your own discreet professional survey in a strictly unprofessional manner. But, remain the "tourist" and do not excite public or official interest in your plans, hopes, or anticipations.

Prior to your second trip, that with your consultants and survey team, obtain as near top introduction as possible to the very Chief of State of the country involved, whether he be President, Dictator, Premier, Monarch, or such.

Now, as immediately after your arrival as may conveniently be arranged, visit this Top Executive in an informal, friendly, interested way. Gradually, during the meeting, inject your project proposal, but in such reserved style and abstract manner as not to reveal excessive enthusiasm, resolve, or eagerness. Emphasize, not the value of the project to you, but the benefit it could convey to the country—Politically, Socially, and Economically. State your agreeableness, as a matter of routine, to investigate the feasibility of the project and report it back to His Excellency.

His Excellency, without great hesitation, will summon several Ministers, perform the necessary amenities by way of introduction, and will detail their assistance to you and your economic survey team. Once you have left the Top Man do not return, socially or otherwise, until you have completed the project's economic study, are relatively certain of its financability, and are prepared to actively and formally negotiate the concession.

Now work through your Minister friends, cultivate their confidence, appreciate their cooperation, lean heavily on their experience and advice, and convey to them the impression that your decision and future action will be theirs. These Ministers, if you are fortunate, will be most important to your success for they can either supply you or not with the factors which will weigh your project in the balance of positive or negative. In the field or in the Capital, they will be indispensable to you and the greater your demands on their time, energies, and facilities, strangely the greater will be their cooperation. Make your plan their plan, and sweat—sweat in your formulations for the advancement of their economy.

At this point it will not be amiss, and it should be well taken in the spirit in which the advice is given: Be everyone's equal, neither his superior nor inferior.

During the conduct of your economic survey, systematically weigh your requirements—economic and financial—for positive decision to establish the project. Your requirements, of course, will include a valid, legally constituted, long term concession, the recipe for which you have by now already concocted.

As always, in the delicate matter of the concession, you will be informed by your Minister friends that the existing national regulations covering industry and private investment have carefully been devised and promulgated by law. Clearly, they will persist, these generous regulations adapt themselves to your necessity, and in fact would seem to be tailored and made expressly for you.

Gently insist on the very special requirements you must observe if you are to properly and adequately finance your project. After all, emphasize that these are not your requirements—you cannot repeat this too frequently—but those that have been strictly and irrevocably imposed upon you by your rigid bankers. You must inflexibly satisfy these custodians of other people's money, and without such satisfaction, no loan will be forthcoming. Repetition of this theme will have the desired result.

The Chief of State will be quietly but quickly informed, via his Ministers, that you are a most unusual person with equally unusual demands in the shape of a very special concession if the project is to advance. By the time you are ready for concession negotiation, the Chief Executive will be prepared to accommodate you; a little give and take, for sure, but your terms will be approved substantially in their entirety.

Work out concession details and their language with the Ministers, your Financial and Legal Consultants, a local native Attorney for effect, and your Chief Engineer, if desirable. If, after several drafts and what appears to be an impasse has been encountered, do not weaken, vacillate, or threaten—walk out and return to your hotel for a breather and a publicly noted solicitation of the airlines for "next plane out."

If you have been shrewd and know your ground well, you will shortly be summoned to the Executive Suite where the Chief of State will reassure you of eventual complete accord and approval of your requirements. Solutions must not appear too simple, public criticism must not be incited, and—above all—personal prides must be preserved. The psychologist classifies it all as "defensive mechanism." You should be keen enough to sense it and sufficiently intelligent to understand.

The next summons will be from the Ministers and in a flash you will have your concession—with coffee.

An official reception usually follows the signing ceremonies and, prior to your departure for home base, you will wisely reciprocate the occasion. Make this *your* golden and precious opportunity for personally meeting key Cabinet Ministers, elements of the Armed Command, Secret Police, and such other components of Government as may be useful and valuable to you at the later date.

SOME IMPORTANT DONT's!

In your concession, DON'T:
1. Establish a schedule of work with completion dates.
2. Commit yourself to grants, royalties, or road subsidies.
3. Permit "fiscalization" of your financial records.
4. Authorize government inspection of work in progress, administrative procedures, or operations—other than as a courtesy gesture.
5. Employ labor, appoint executives or managers, or retain professionals (lawyers, accountants, engineers, etc.) on government remonstrances or those of any of its officials.
6. Restrict your purchases of materials and supplies to only those of national origin, or if not of national origin, to sources of native import and distribution. Freely purchase and import at your own option.
7. Encumber your directorate with politicians, officials, or their appointees. This is outright and outrageous courtship with disaster.

30

8. Submit disputes, labor and otherwise, solely to government "arbitration."

9. Engage yourself, your agents, or your employees to propagandize the government administration in power. This courts ill will when administrations change.

10. Lobby externally, no matter how justifiably. Speak well but not outright.

11. Distribute your product through channels other than those of your own free choice.

12. Undertake an entire program of social reform. If immediate changes are to be made, the change must be in you!

6 Financing: Part I

Financing your project will require the skilled work of educated, experienced experts, viz.:
1. The Financial Consultant
2. The Legal Counsellor
3. The Consultant Engineers

Before you solicit in earnest and with serious intent, the capital funds to engineer and construct your project, you must equip yourself with the "FEASIBILITY REPORT." This report, specifically undertaken and prepared for your project, must substantiate and support your loan request. It will commonly be divided into three main sections:

1 ECONOMICS OF THE PROJECT

a) Descriptive.
b) Raw Material Supply.
c) Labor.
d) Cost of Production.
e) Market.
f) Transportation.
g) Taxes and Duties.
h) Management.

2   ENGINEERING

a)   Plant Site Investigation and Location.
b)   Specifications and Preliminary Lay Out.
c)   Project Costs.
d)   Flow Chart of Capital Funds Utilization.

3   FINANCIAL

a)   General Narrative.
b)   Pro-forma Financial Statements.
c)   Application of Funds Statement.
d)   Formal Report.
e)   Loan Application.

1   ECONOMICS OF THE PROJECT

Much of this work was accomplished on your first official trip, excluding the tourist jaunt, when you conducted the survey for economics and general financabilitiy of the project. Very probably sufficient comprehensive data was accumulated then to now incorporate it in the Feasibility Report without necessity of making additional travel to complete it.

a/   Descriptive

Word picture the Project, its need to the general economy of the nation, how it will serve and be served, its function and general planned operation in relation to the overall national structure, political and economic.

b / Raw Material Supply

You know your requirements and, by now, you must be aware of their sources of best supply, native origin or import, or mixed.

Emphasize cheapness of local supplies and justify imports on the basis of your *finished* product cost vs. its imported counterpart.

c / Labor

Labor is an impressive factor and its long range trend and influence must be favorably predicted if financability is to be correctly gauged and presented.

This is no real obstacle, however, because of available surplus labor in your project territory. It just simply must be reliable, sober, and competent within its own uneducated confines. Your imported technicians, if worth their salt and your employ, will easily recruit, train, and supervise the unskilled forces and, by selection, eventually congregate even the skilled crews.

d / Cost of Production

Calculate your unit costs of production more accurately than you did in the field, and scale them to U.S.A. costs for similar production, allowing for substantial differentials in the elements of labor, etc.

e / Market

If you were sharp in the field, you now have a committed market in your vest pocket—the concession.

f/ Transportation

This you have already surveyed and charted for distances and routes, actually siting your plant at a point radial to all choice consumer centers. Prove it!

g/ Taxes and Duties

This normally objectionable matter will lighten your banker's heart when you disclose your total and complete exemption on long term basis—in proof, your concession.

h/ Management

Good administration is hard to come by, but it will come to you if satisfactorily compensated.

Import your needed talent, highly paid and bonused; adopt a training program and replace the imports in time with local vintage, as and when it matures.

Keep the politicians out. Their influence should be tempered, if countenanced at all.

2   ENGINEERING STUDY

This responsibility definitely, and without argument, belongs to an outstanding firm of Consultant Engineers. The Feasibility Report is intended primarily for the bankers, and as professionals they demand the professional treatment. Quality, reputation, and performance impress bankers, and these qualifications must be possessed by the firm of Consultants you retain. Good firms command high fees and they are very well worthy of their hire—do not shop or economize here.

a/ Plant Site Investigation and Location

The Consultant Engineers will check-out the plant site you may have tentatively selected or they will independently select one best situated for your project. The principal factors they will determine: proximity to water supply, presence of good soil and foundation conditions, availability of fuel and power, access to transportation routes, markets, etc.

b/ Specifications and Preliminary Layout

The project capacities, plant specifications, and laying out the physical plant are time consuming and expensive but cannot be by-passed, short cut, or omitted.

c/ Project Costs

Sets of preliminary costs will be prepared, assembled, and interpreted into a solid presentation of financial figures which feed into the loan application.

d/ Flow Chart of Capital Funds Utilization

Not all the proceeds of the loan will be required at once but will be expended in ratio to engineering performance and physical plant construction. Proper estimate of requirements will materially diminish loan interest expense and thereby reduce capital expenditure.

3 FINANCIAL

a/ General Narrative

This will supplement general descriptive as supplied by the engineering force. Into this inject the political, social, and economic position and potential of the project country, correlating the project, what it will accomplish, immediately and long range, intrinsically and extrinsically.

b/ Pro-forma Financial Statements

Estimate financial condition of project in pro-forma style, with conservative forecast of earnings, reflecting surplus additions fully capable of absorbing debt amortizations.

Project your operations, year by year, at least for total period of capital indebtedness, assuring capacity to absorb maximum production and other charges, interest expense and contingency reserve provisions, with net transfers to earned surplus not only adequate to cover loan amortizations but to provide handsome return on investment as well.

c/ Application of Funds Statement

Schedule, in conjunction with engineering requirements, the progressive utilizations of capital funds to be borrowed. This will substantially reduce interest expense, while the project is in engineering and under construction, and thereby will eliminate wasteful capital expenditure.

d/ Formal Report

All the foregoing procedures culminate in this documentary which blends economic, engineering, and financial surveys and studies into

38

one forceful presentation which must substantiate and support your capital loan application.

Through this work should be interwoven a pattern of guarantees which will collateralize the loan to the entire and immediate satisfaction of the bankers.

e/ Loan Application

The loan offering is finally prepared, incorporated within the report, and presented to the bankers.

Your financial negotiations follow.

Good luck!

7 Financing: Part II

Financing locales, of prominent interest, are to be found in North America, specifically the United States, Continental Europe, and to a limited extent in Japan, with modest generation possible in England.

The United States, often cited as the pocketbook of the world (and it is), should offer the very finest in foreign financing facilities and, certainly, it is nobly and expertly equipped to perform with maximum results. However, the indications are—and for some have been—that financing of foreign projects may be accomplished with considerably greater ease in Europe. The reasons for this are too complex, political, and controversial for the author to become engaged in or attempt their explanation.

Suffice it to say, there is a weakness in the structure of foreign financing by United States institutions (non-government). This much is definite. There also is, relatively speaking in comparison with Europe, a decided deficiency in *methods* employed by the United States Government to promote and encourage foreign project development by its Nationals—as comparisons will confirm. Both the structural weakness and the methods deficiency are subject to correction, and unless such is effected, United States private enterprise abroad, U.S.A. contractors, manufacturers, and suppliers, U.S.A. financial institutions, and the power and prestige of the United States itself will irrevocably and substantially suffer; as in-

41

full zest to your "problem" that one would imagine it was their own.

Of course, should you utilize French or Italian financing, you must expect that your contractors, manufacturers, and suppliers will be of the same national origin as your loan funds. This is no more than fair and, truly, it is the invigorating motive of export market development that so inspires the French and Italian financiers. This, good reader, is the key difference between the United States banking fraternity and that of its French and Italian counterparts. The French and the Italians have tremendous and awesome national urge for development abroad, *and they enjoy government subsidy*; the United States brethren have not the one nor do they enjoy the other!

Prior to maturing your negotiations too ripely with the European banker of your choice, select from his current list of customers one who is a general contractor of importance, as also an engineering firm of national reputation. Bring principals of these companies into the area of discussion and negotiation, inject local manufacturers of merit, and persuade a weighty member of their government to assist in the general conduct of the entire affair. Capital budget may be revised, as European costs generally are less than U.S.A., estimated results of operations could be modified for technical reasons of manufacture, specifications changed, even market of product happily extended to the country of loan. This not infrequently does happen.

If your Feasibility Report substantially withstands the rigorous check it will surely receive and the project is conceded sound and financable, arrangements will be made by the bank for appropriate action by itself and by government agencies, for extension to you of required credit and funds for engineering and constructing your enterprise.

The French or Italian bank, if you are qualified and correct, will actually discharge the necessary formalities for you with its government, in your favor and that of the national engineers, general contractors, manufacturers, and suppliers involved.

Red tape will be present but it will be reduced to a minimum and, during the period of transition from conference table to official execution of financing, you will be considerably and agreeably occupied in technical matters of your own concern.

In connection with your relationship with European bankers, it not only is good courtesy but it is most impressive, as well, to deliver to these gentlemen a letter of introduction from your prime bank back home. Bankers, as do we all, appreciate the well referenced individual and you cannot afford to be an exception. If convenient and possible, it is excellent practice to have your home banker call his foreign counterpart, by transatlantic phone, introduce you over the wire, explain your mission briefly, time of arrival, hour of appointment, and any deadline imposed. This simple and tactful operation defrosts you prior to arrival and assures a most warm reception when you show in person.

It will be profitable to take note that in the system of French banking particularly, there exists an impressive array of formidable banks, each of which specializes in a world area: European countries other than France, also Asia, Africa, Latin America, etc. Many of these institutions boast their own large financial establishments on the scene of their foreign activities and do not necessarily rely on local correspondent banks for representation. The ease of negotiation and operation with these French entities can readily be understood. Not only are they fully capable of negotiating and carrying your project loan, but they most competently can and will participate in project planning and actual operation. The same, but to a lesser extent, can be said of the Italian institutions. In the author's opinion and experience, however, while the Italian bank has not the magnitude of the French, it does show promise of closing the gap with considerable speed.

Private banking groups are in goodly number in France and are quite alert, responsive, and financially strong and powerful. Their interests outside of France are extensive, diversified, and aggressively receptive to expansion. Many of them operate through channels of

of your success in securing good financing with completely positive results in the field.

Then, too, the Project Concession is a rich asset not cheaply possessed, and a substantial outlay of time and money must be invested to secure it.

Other expense factors will occur and many must be defrayed prior to any loan negotiations and even before completion of the Feasibility Report—sub-contracts for soil tests and preliminary foundation survey, local legal expense, inland transportation usually by air charter, civil engineering, topographical charting, and other major items not previously contemplated.

To conclude, the funds can be made available for the financable project, either in the United States with U.S.A. contractors, contingent on the force and character of circumstances surrounding you, your project, and the country of your industrial choice; or, they may await your negotiation in Europe.

In either case, do not overlook the extreme importance of your passport to financing—The Feasibility Report!

8 Post Financing

Presuming that your financing has been completely and satisfactorily accomplished, three important maneuvers must be executed:
1. Corporate.
2. Banking Accommodations.
3. Contractor Relations.

1   CORPORATE

In establishing your foreign corporation, by all means be counseled jointly by your foreign and domestic attorneys. Together they will devise the legal structure best equipped to shelter project operations, protect your personal interests, *and deploy for potentials.*

The corporate franchise should be both broad and specific, limiting to poachers and unlimited itself, providing for current requirements and expansive for future. It should very definitely, somewhere appropriately in the text, absorb in detail the very wording of your legally constituted Concession, but it should not be restricted to the articles thereof. It should even be foresighted enough to countenance "inside—outside" operations, and to include "everything but the kitchen sink"—and throw that in too.

The franchise, when ready, should be delivered directly to the National Government for specific, explicit and registered approval, and then should be submitted to the processes of constitutional law, with official act of notarization in full context, and complete publication in the Government Gazette. All this may require months of patient, exhausting labor and a not insignificant expenditure of money, but it someday may yield unpredictable and substantial returns by way of commercial survival, competitive edge, and enjoyment of rights not foreseen, viz., royalties, licenses, claims, etc.

The by-laws applicable to your foreign corporation could nicely be the routine standard set, modified and amended to your pleasure.

One word, though, about your Directorate:—appoint it wisely and for commercial acumen, not political expediency. It could be embarrassing, and hazardous, once a political appointment has been made to dismiss it, or to retain it under a change in government administration.

2   BANKING ACCOMMODATIONS

Your principal institution will be that of loan origin and with this bank you will manage your system of disbursements during the construction period, income and expenditure in later actual production operations, amortization and interest treatment, working capital, crop loans if applicable, short term financings, and such other of the project's fiscal necessities as may pertain.

By all means, though, arrange with your local native bank the methods for transfers of funds, covering of payrolls and tight squeeze situations which inevitably occur. This local bank could very well operate as a correspondent of your lending bank and the relations thereby created and cemented could redound to your benefit.

3   CONTRACTOR RELATIONS

The method of financing employed by you will dictate or permit your choice of contractors.

Prior to loan negotiations with the foreign bank, it is an accepted policy that you name your contractors and suppliers of heavy machinery and equipment. It has already been specified that they generally must be resident of country of loan origin, otherwise no loan motive will exist on the part of the lending bank or its government. Furthermore, it is academic to say that the lending bank will favor its own customers in this direction.

Hence, once your financing has been made available to you, it is a relatively simple affair to negotiate definitive contracts for the engineering and construction of your enterprise. The bank will undoubtedly assign one of its directors, and also its legal department, to represent its interests in all such negotiations and a really harmonious and quite efficient relationship will develop and continue throughout.

In addition, the bank's staff will be found freely accessible to you, and your needs in many areas will be formidably and uncomplainingly serviced to joint satisfaction of all concerned. This outstanding service particularly holds true in legal-governmental clearances, export documentations, currency exchanges, labor situations, priorities, expedition of shipping, insurance, performance bonds, etc.

On the other hand, should you have been recipient of United States financing—private, commercial, or government agency—your freedom in selection of contractors is very nearly complete. Your contractors must simply qualify with the lender and little or no restraint will be imposed beyond this.

Qualification may vary in style and application but the following components usually satisfy:
1. Well Established.
2. Efficiently Organized.
3. Experienced.

4. Accomplished.
5. Financially Valid.
6. Ethically Acceptable.

1   WELL ESTABLISHED

The contractor should not be a new arrival in the industry but is expected to present a background of operation for a reasonable period of years.

Many of our old name contractors have disappeared from the foreign field and the survival of others is uncertain. This is no reflection on these former and contemporary grand old giants; but it does give indictment to the forces and circumstances contributing to their demise or, if they still exist, to the threat that could destroy them.

World War II historic fact bears eloquent testimony and honest tribute to the courage, ability and heroic accomplishment of the great corps of engineers and general contractors—U.S.A. vintage— who from 1941 through 1945 contributed in immeasurable value to the survival and subsequent victory of the United States of America. Their professional qualifications, totally outstanding performances, and recorded miracles of engineering and construction, under the impossible conditions encountered and faced, have rarely been equalled and possibly will never be surpassed by others. Certainly their monumental feats of 1941–1945 should not now be an epitaph to their past, but an incentive for United States Government guarantee of their future. They rate no less. And neither does the United States of America!

United States engineering and general contractors of any substantial proportions, available for foreign work, number too few and these "too few" will be the sole survivors who can qualify as "Well Established."

Rather than saying "Well Done" to those who have disappeared into history, it would be far more heartening to voice "Welcome Back." *Only U.S. Government subsidy, in competition with that of Europe, can do this.* It is hoped that the Industry will read this and add more than its solemn "Amen".

2   EFFICIENTLY ORGANIZED

The "Well Established" contractor will be high geared with a competent, precision calibered, industrious, and reliable staff, the nucleus of which, at least, will average long tenure of employment.

Hiring practices, policies, and media of employment have been tested and proven without need for experiment or innovation.

Official responsibilities, jurisdictions and administrations, with prompt decision, are clearly defined, located, and exercised.

Various services: purchasing, sub-contracting, etc., are conducted in professional, bona-fide, and orderly manner through specialized divisions.

Fiscal, as well as general, conduct of business are managed by select and qualified officers and personnel.

3   EXPERIENCED

Seasoned, broad, and successful performance for clients over long period of mature operation are the elements here.

If your project is of a specialized nature, seek the best qualified specialist in that particular technical area. What he cannot perform within his own specialty, he will honestly sub-contract out to others better qualified.

4 ACCOMPLISHED

"Nothing succeeds like success."

Obtain the performance record of the general contractor, scan the substantial projects he has completed and even those in progress, the names of his clients in each respective case. Confirm directly with these clients the degree of their satisfaction with Contractor.

Have your domestic bank solicit similar information from general and trade sources.

Accomplishment simply means record of successful completion with desired results.

5 FINANCIALLY VALID

Balance sheet stature, earned surplus strength, heavy cash position, liquidity—these add up to financial eligibility and are mandatory requirements in your choice of Contractor.

Do not underestimate surplus and cash importance. You will pay for your job, another customer may not, and you could suffer disastrous results, performance bond notwithstanding.

Validity also demands that the Contractor be bondable for performance, including completion, and insurable for other coverages that may be required by you or your banker, or suggested by your own insurance agent or broker.

The Contractor should obligate himself to periodically provide you with certified financial statements, not only of his own condition but likewise that of your job. Presumably progress payments, ratioed to job completion, will be observed, with down payment on execution of the definitive contract. The Contractor will be accustomed to normal accounting procedures for this and your banker will insist on documentation of all expenditures, so be forewarned and properly prepared.

Ethics apply to individuals as well as companies. Unfortunately, in one way, the corporate body is a composite of individuals and the weakness of one, in the critical public eye, may destroy the strength of all the others.

What we do good generally goes unnoticed and unapplauded; one slip, though, and the entire world would condemn.

With this in mind, and conscious that one worm does not destroy the entire crop, consider the entire reputation of the Contractor and do not isolate your judgment in one criticism.

The Contractor who maintains his name, style, and operation in dignity and with honesty, is the rule not the exception.

Presumably, the Consultant Engineers who served in the conduct of the economic study and compilation of data for the Feasibility Report will continue in your employ as project engineers. Since you now have obtained necessary financing, largely based on the success of their labors and skill, it would seem unreasonable to change professional services. Hence, no good reasons to the contrary, the best interests of your project realization will be served by holding intact your original forces: Consultant Engineers, Legal Counsellor, and Financial Consultant.

This being the case, complete reliance should be placed in your Consultant Engineers' selection of General Contractor, and Project Engineers if especially required. The Consultant Engineers are far better qualified and more experienced than could be you in this respect and certainly they are immediately well acquainted with the requirements of your job and the Contractors most suitable to build it.

Your Consultant Engineers, also, are skilled in bidding and contracting methods and procedures. Together with your Financial and Legal forces they will negotiate superior contracting instruments not otherwise available through either your own efforts or those comparative stranger to the job. Be sensible, not boss!

The Eleventh Commandment to observe, however, is: Choose your original Consultant Engineers for better, not worse!

The author would like to add: "And that applies to your Financial Consultant and Legal Counsellor, too.

9 Conclusion

There *does* exist a refreshingly new world for Industrial Conquest in this rusting, debauched, and decadent old world that we have accepted with frustration and in despair this mid-twentieth century of "progress."

This new world lies in the New Nations that have lately been born to our stagnant, regressive is more accurate, civilization. It situates also in the forgotten areas of many Older Nations which have suffered tediously and sadly through long periods of wanton neglect, indifference, and even abuse.

We have witnessed program after program, listened to lip-service upon lip-service, read account by account of the vast social benefits and human development projects which in one year, five years, ten years would raise living standards and bring prosperity to those, the so-called "underprivileged nations." The record of results is not worth a countdown.

Philosophies may freely be exchanged in the matter of diagnosis, prognosis, and treatment, but meanwhile the patient cruelly suffers and too frequently is dying of vicious political or ideological cancer.

Industry has always been the classic cure for unemployment, inevitably it has bulkheaded and cultured society, permanently it brings improved standards of living, as also hope and peace. Industry, yes; controlled industry, No.

With this concept, and the welcome extended, industrialists and investors of good intent have not only moral obligation, but profitable motive as well, to extend their practical and potent capacities to the development of the New Nations and the re-development of many of the Old.

Understandable caution, fear, and even terror may inhibit expression of positive action by many industrialists; culpable ignorance, own up to it, is the real deterrent.

The nightmare of Cuba lurks heavily and disturbingly, fogs of ignorance shroud facts, and successfully camouflaged bias distorts reports of atrocities, rebellions and political coups. Border incident is heaped upon border incident, gripping tales of "bogeymen" are circulated as freely as Grimm's, with considerably more substance and far less veracity. Political changes in government occur with unclocklike precision and economic sanction is hurled about with style reminiscent of a sand-lot ball game.

The confusion, chaos, and near insanity of this hodgepodge are calculated to penetrate the industrial intelligence and keep virgin the potency of even the most prolific industrialist.

This is a deplorable and sick situation which only integrity, ability, and active resolve, all on the part of the industrialist, can cure. It requires a rugged determination to win, distinguished fortitude and courage not to lose. Win you can, and lose you need not, if you have the will and the relentless desire to profit, not only for your own account but also for those for whom you develop and build.

Do not say that there are no real opportunities, that they exist only in fancy and not in fact. This is the evasion of those who think conveniently and not productively.

The author particularly is objectively conscious of "New Nations," and even "Older," where industrial development in specialized areas offers such ripe opportunities as to satisfy the industrial appetite of the most exacting gourmet. In every respect they qualify for sound investment but they deserve maturity of conscience, superior intent, and humaneness of purpose, all conducive not only

58

to the development of a People but, since we must be selfish, to munificent and profitable investment return as well. These opportunities are not isolated cases, they are duplicated many times over in other and widely distributed regions of the world. The point is, they *are* there.

For the most part, the opportunities presented in and by these "New" and "Older" Countries are unparalleled, for permanency of operation and magnitude of profits. And yet they are neglected because of mass hypnotism exercised upon the industrialist and the investor by propaganda, lurid reports, and political sanctions which are perennially issued and rescinded without logic.

All this does not destroy the validity of existence of rich territories for industrial expansion and development. It emphatically accentuates the need for industrial action in positive, not negative style. It is then for the industrialist and the investor to seize the initiative, now by choice, *as they must eventually through necessity,* and progress with the weapons of their industry where neither the sword has conquered nor political contest won.

Be aggressive but never forget, above all else, be *selective!*

The Author

Ambrose J. Hartnett is a citizen of the United States of America, born in St. Louis, Missouri, June 22, 1911.

An executive international banker for many years, he has engaged in financial work since 1934, with wide experience in the foreign field.

During World War II, he served from September 1941 to March 1946 as a Line Officer in the United States Navy and was responsible for devising and establishing many of the major financial procedures observed in the Department, Washington, D.C.

He holds a degree from Fordham University, and is an accredited C.P.A., State of New York.

His other works, in addition to numerous industrial and financial plans of development and expansion, include *An Aid to Project Financing in Foreign Countries*, *Breakthrough for Haiti*, and *An International Plan for United States Banking and Industry* to be published in the fall of 1964.